Flip-flops and Shades on Thassos - 3rd Edition

This is the 3rd edition of this book which is set on the paradise Greek holiday island of Thassos which is in the Northern Aegean Sea close to the warm Mediterranean blue azure sea. We will explore the island in words, photographs and my artwork.

by Norfolk Watercolour Artist - Alan R. Massen
Published in Great Britain by Rainbow Publications UK

First Published in 2016 by Rainbow Publications UK
2nd Edition Published in 2019 by Rainbow Publications UK
3rd Edition Published in 2020 by Rainbow Publications UK

Copyright © 2020 Alan R. Massen

The moral right of Alan R. Massen to be identified as the author of this work has been asserted in accordance with the UK Copyright, Designs and Patents Act of 1988. All rights reserved. No part of this book may be reproduced, or stored in a retrieval system, or transmitted in any form or by any means, electronic, mechanical, photocopying, recording, or otherwise, without the prior written permission of both the author and the above publisher of this book All imagery and illustrations

© Alan R. Massen

Neither the publisher nor the author can accept liability for the use of any of the materials, methods or information recommended in this book or for any consequences arising out of their use, nor can they be held responsible for any errors or omissions that may be found in the text or may occur at a future date as a result of changes in rules, laws or equipment All manufacturers, sellers, product names and services identified in this book are used in editorial fashion and for the benefit of such companies with no intention of any infringement of trademarks. No such use or the use of any trade name is intended to convey endorsement or other affiliation with this book. Every effort has been made to obtain the necessary permissions with reference to copyright material, both illustrative and quoted. We apologize for any omissions in this respect and will be pleased to make the appropriate acknowledgements in any future edition.

Paperback Edition ISBN 978-0-9933962-8-1
Typeset in Minion Pro

Published in Great Britain by Rainbow Publications UK

About the Author

Alan was born in the city of Norwich in the county of Norfolk, England in November 1949. When Alan was still a teenager he started painting whilst attending art classes in Norwich. In his mid-teens he had two paintings accepted for a National Art Exhibition held in London and other major UK cities. Alan spent most of his working life as a professional Health and Safety Advisor and rarely picked up a paint brush until he, his wife Susie and daughter Ginny (his other daughter Mandy is married and lives with her husband Adrian in Sheffield) moved out of the city of Norwich into the countryside in 1993. They moved to a little village called East Lexham in the heart of Norfolk. The village was very peaceful and pretty. This helped inspire Alan to take up watercolour painting once again.

In 2004 they moved to another small West Norfolk village near Downham Market where they still live today. In 2008 Alan had to retire due to ill health (bad knees) and whilst he still painted regularly he began to spend more and more time gardening. In 2013 his wife Susie suggested that he kept a gardening diary to record his adventures in the garden and capture the changing seasons, animals, birds and the successes and failures of being a gardener he encountered. By the following year Susie suggested that he should write a book from his diary and include illustrations of both the garden and his artwork. In 2014 Alan's first book was published by Creative Gateway called **"Retiring to the Garden – Year One"**. This proved such a success that Alan decided to follow this up with his second book called **"Retiring into a Rainbow"** featuring his watercolour paintings.

He then in 2015 published **"Retiring to Our Garden – Year Two"** published this time by Rainbow Publications UK. He then re-issued his first two books this time in a **"Second Edition"**. Also published by Rainbow Publications UK. His next planned publications are: **"Skiathos a Greek Island Paradise"** and **"Norfolk the County of my Birth"** and **"Ibiza Island of Dreams"**. He has recently completed four new books which are entitled: **"Art Inspired by a Rainbow"**, **"Flip-flops and Shades on Thassos"**, **"Majorca Island in the Sun"**, and finally **"Mardle and a Troshin' in Norfolk"** and in 2020 he published this new 3rd edition book on Thassos which will be published by Rainbow Publications UK in the near future.

I hope you enjoy this my latest book on the Greek Island of Thassos…

Books by Alan R. Massen

Retiring to the Garden Year 1 - Paperback
Retiring into a Rainbow - Paperback
Retiring into a Rainbow - 1st Edition - My Favourite Artwork 2020 - 1st Edition
Retiring to our Garden Year one - 1st & 2nd Editions
Retiring to our Garden Year two - 1st & 2nd & 3rd Editions
Retiring into a Rainbow - 1st & 2nd Editions
Skiathos a Greek Island Paradise - 1st & 2nd & 3rd Editions
Norfolk the County of my Birth - 1st & 2nd & 3rd Editions
Art Inspired by a Rainbow - 1st & 2nd & 3rd Editions
Ibiza Island of Dreams - 1st & 2nd Editions
Majorca Island in the Sun - 1st & 2nd Editions
Flip-Flops and Shades on Thassos - 1st & 2nd & 3rd Editions
Mardle and a Troshin' in Norfolk - 1st & 2nd Editions
England the Country of my Birth - 1st & 2nd Editions
Mousehole the Cornish Jewel - 1st & 2nd & 3rd Editions
Sunshades & Flip-Flops on Kefalonia - 1st & 2nd & 3rd Editions
Shades & Flip-Flops on Zakynthos - 1st & 2nd & 3rd Editions
Trips into my Minds Eye - 1st & 2nd & 3rd & 4th Editions
Corfu and Mainland Greece - 1st & 2nd & 3rd Editions
Crete and the Island of Santorini - 1st & 2nd & 3rd Editions
Cyprus - Pyramids - Holy Land - 1st & 2nd & 3rd Editions
Greek Islands in the Sun - 1st & 2nd & 3rd Editions
Being Greek - 1st & 2nd & 3rd Editions

E-books and Booklets:

Retiring to the Garden Yr 1 - Retiring into a Rainbow - My Art 1997 - 2018 - Skiathos a Greek Paradise Island
My Norfolk - My Greece - My England - My Team - My Skiathos - My Art - My Album of Visual Art
My Village - Greece Land of Gods and Men - Norfolk Wildlife - Civilisation (Empires of the Past)
Boudica Queen of the Iceni - Roman Britain

Susie and Alan…

Copyright © 2020 - Alan R. Massen
Published in Great Britain by Rainbow Publications UK

Books by the same Author

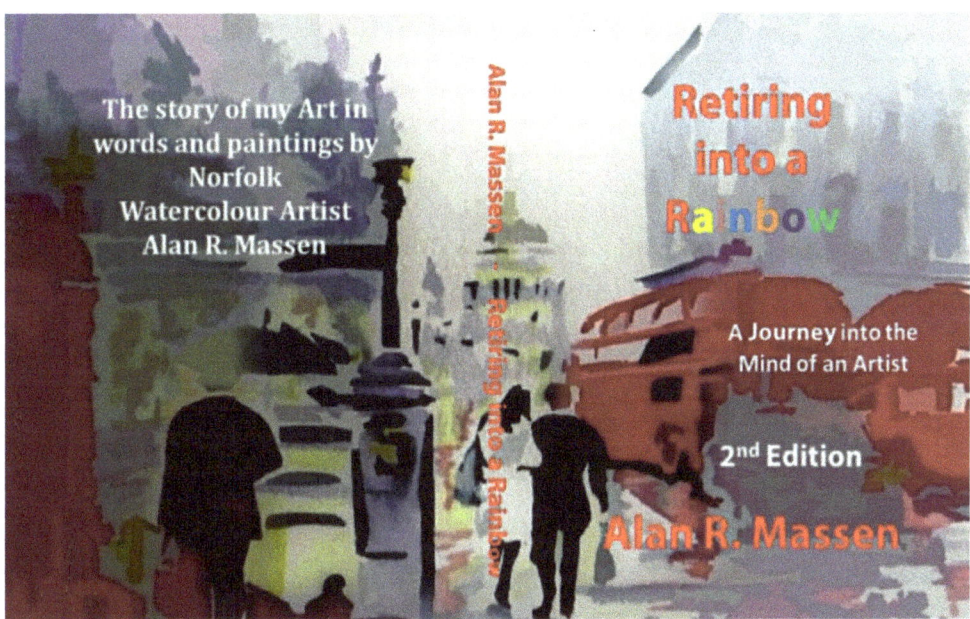

Published 1st Edition by Creative Gateway and 2nd Edition by Rainbow Publications UK

Books by the same Author

Published by Rainbow Publications UK

Books by the same Author

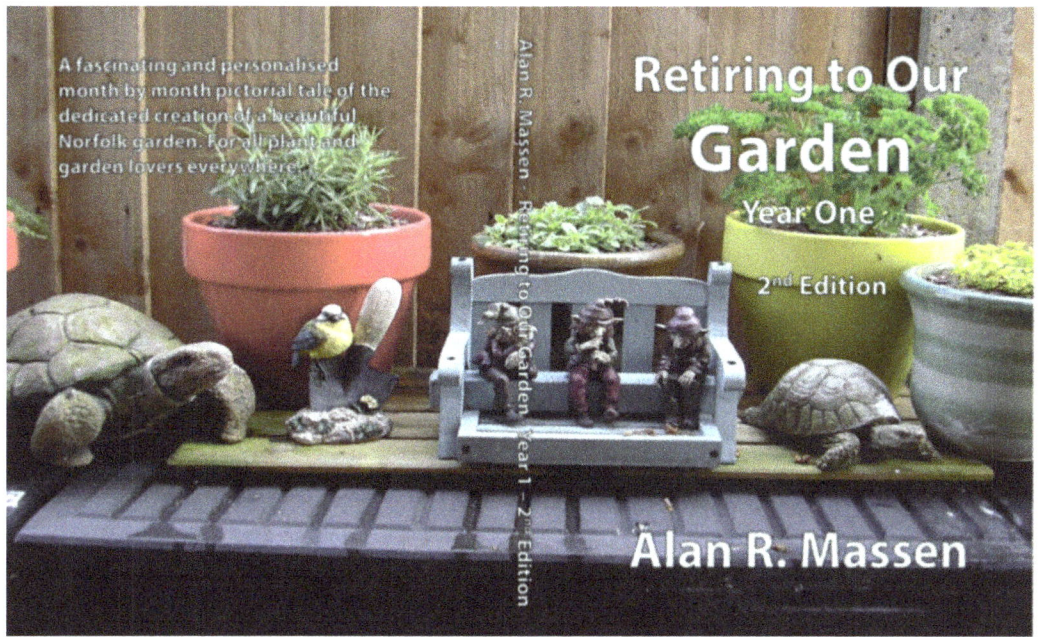

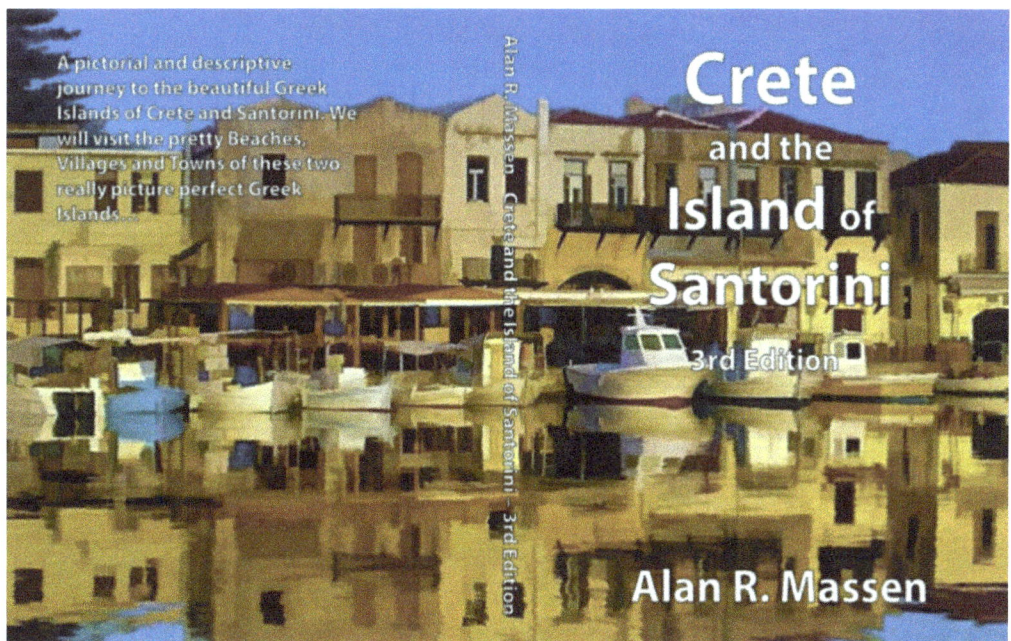

Published by Rainbow Publications UK

Books by the same Author

Published by Rainbow Publications UK

Books by the same Author

Published by Rainbow Publications UK

Books by the same Author

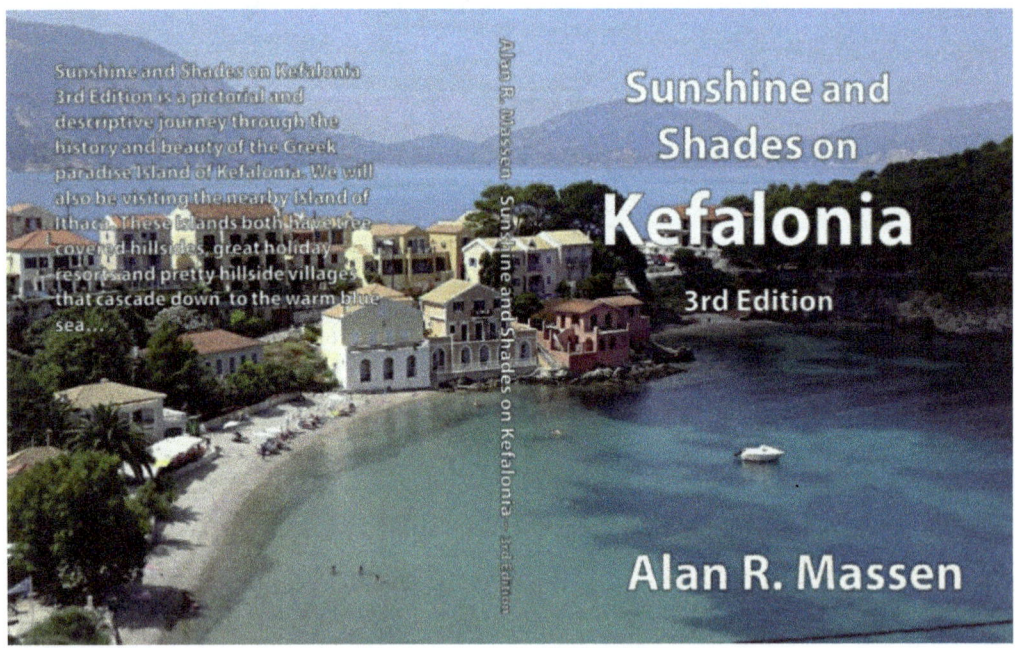

Published in Great Britain by Rainbow Publications UK

Books by the same Author

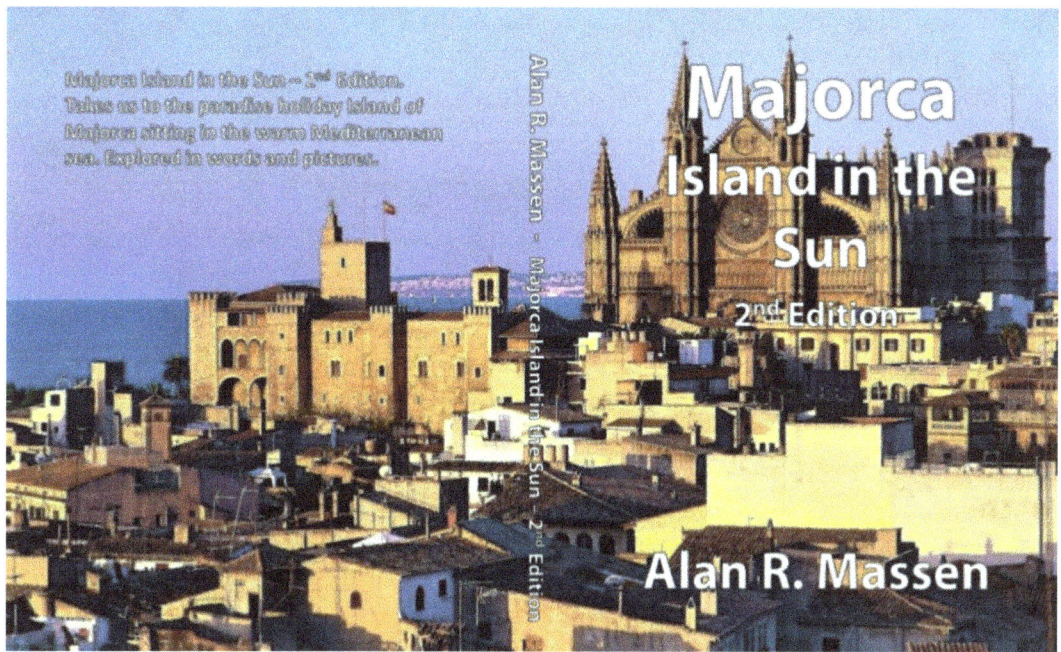

by Norfolk Watercolour Artist - Alan R. Massen
Published in Great Britain by Rainbow Publications UK

Books by the same Author

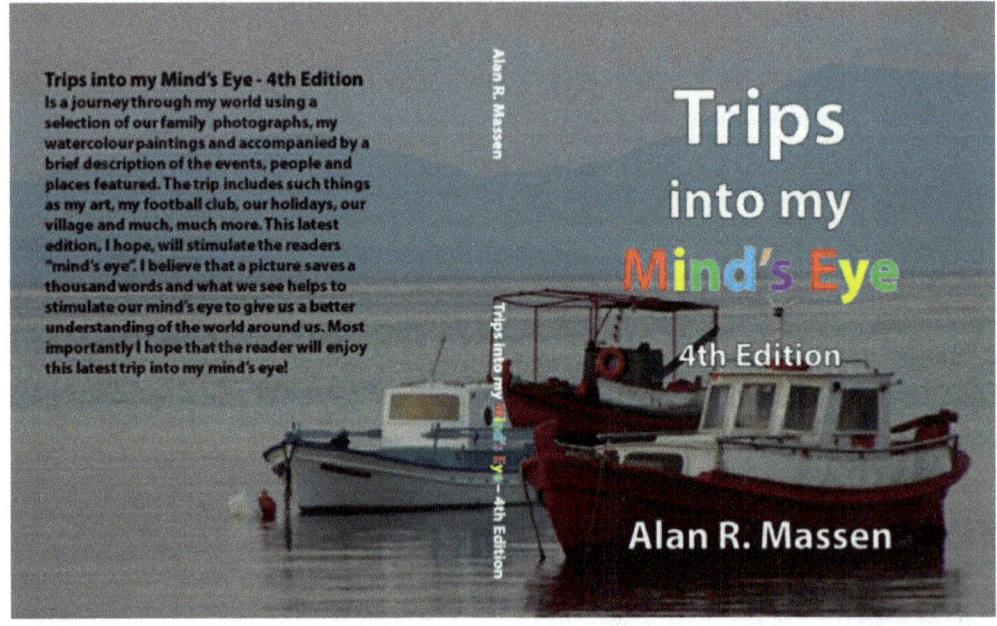

by Norfolk Watercolour Artist - Alan R. Massen
Published in Great Britain by Rainbow Publications UK

Books by the same Author

by Norfolk Watercolour Artist - Alan R. Massen
Published in Great Britain by Rainbow Publications UK

Books by the same Author

by Norfolk Watercolour Artist - Alan R. Massen
Published in Great Britain by Rainbow Publications UK

Dedication

Welcome to my book called **"Flip-flops and Shades on Thassos".** I would like to dedicate this book to all those people worldwide who have lost loved ones during the recent terrible Coronavirus pandemic of 2020. All those who have left us will always be remembered and live on in our hearts and minds as we remember all of the love, support and smiles that they shared with us during their lifetimes. I would also like to thank the wonderful, dedicated and brave doctors, nurses and all of the other essential workers who put their own lives at risk to help others during this tragedy. Their bravery has been an inspiration to us all during this awful time and we thank each and to every one of them. **THANK YOU**…

Susie and Alan…

This book features the Greek paradise Island of Thassos and I would like to dedicate this book to our very good friends Alistair, Issy, Karl, Anna, Andrew and Lynn who like us also love their holidays in the Mediterranean.

Susie and Alan say **CHEERS** and we thank all of our friends for their company both home and abroad over the last twenty five years.

Welcome to Flip-flops and shades on Thassos I hope you enjoy this my latest book…

Contents

Introduction to Thassos……………………	1
The History of Thassos …………………..	6
The Geography of Thassos ………………	21
Facts About Thassos…………………….	23
Out and About on Thassos……………...	27
Exploring Thassos..……………………...	32
Thassos Town ………...…..……………	84
Thassos in Colour …………...…………..	90
Acknowledgement …………………….	202

Copyright © 2020 Alan R. Massen

Introduction to Thassos

Alan on Thassos…

Thassos is the most northerly of the Greek islands in the Aegean island group and it lies just off the Macedonian coast in the north-east of mainland Greece. Fabulously wealthy in ancient times, thanks to large deposits of gold and marble, Thassos nowadays lies outside the top league of Greek holiday islands but it still has much to offer the visitor. We have been there for our summer holidays on several occassions and enjoyed it very much…

Introduction to Thassos

Most tourist arrive at Alexandra the Great International airport in Kavala which is on the mainland of Greece. Then it is a short ferry journey over to Thassos. The first time we went to Thassos we were not sure how the ferry journey would be after having a long days journey to get there. As it happens we loved it and it really added to the holiday experience for us. To reach the accommodation at the resorts many visitors use the local taxis or the coaches provided by the tour operators. An excellent coast road almost rings the whole island, providing easy access to the many sandy beaches that pepper the attractive coastline. Strangely, Thassos fails to feature in many holiday brochures so it is something of a hidden gem and spared the usual holiday crowds that mar some of the other Greek islands…

Introduction to Thassos

Makryammos Beach…

The pine trees come right down to the shoreline on Thassos. The extensive pine trees that carpet most of Thassos have led to it being rightly dubbed the ' Emerald Isle' of Greece. We enjoyed the shade the pine trees gave when we sat under them on the beaches.

Giola lagoon

The beaches, mostly sandy, are dotted all around the coast with a wide variety on offer, from large, deep beaches with plenty of facilities to small, idyllic hideaway coves. Side roads branch inland to charming hill villages and to extensive tracts of dense woodland which have many walking trails in them to enjoy…

Introduction to Thassos

Thassos may be off the main tourist trail but regular ferries run from Keramouti which is only a 10 minute ride from the airport at Kavala (Kavala Town is featured above). Thassos is in the Northern Aegean Sea and is close to the coast of Thrace and the plain of the river Nestos but is geographically part of Macedonia…

Introduction to Thassos

Thassos is the northernmost Greek island, and twelfth largest by area. Thassos is also the name of the largest town of the island (also known as Limenas Thasou, "Harbour of Thassos"), situated on the northern side of the island, opposite the mainland and about 10 kilometres (6 miles) from Keramoti on the Greek mainland…

The History of Thassos

Alexander the Great

Lying close to the coast of Eastern Macedonia, Thassos was inhabited from the Palaeolithic period onwards, but the earliest settlement to have been explored in detail is that at Limenaria, where remains from the Middle and Late Neolithic have been found that relate closely to those found on the nearby mainland of Greece…

The History of Thassos

Early Bronze Age remains on the island align it with the Aegean culture of the Cyclades and Sporades, to the south; at Skala Sotiros for example, a small settlement was encircled by a strongly built defensive wall. Even earlier activity is demonstrated by the presence of large pieces of megalithic anthropomorphic stelai built into these walls, which, so far, have no parallels in the Aegean area…

The History of Thassos

Minoan Ship…

There is then a gap in the archaeological record until the end of the Bronze Age c 1100 BC, when the first burials took place at the large cemetery of Kastri in the interior of the island. Here they built tombs covered with a small mound of earth and these were typical until the end of the Iron Age. In the earliest tombs were found a small number of locally imitated Mycenaean pottery vessels, but the majority of the hand-made pottery with incised decoration reflects connections eastwards with Thrace and beyond brought perhaps to the island by Minoan traders!…

The History of Thassos

The island of Thassos was colonised at an early date by the Phoenicians, attracted probably by its gold mines; they founded a temple to the god Melqart, whom the Greeks identified as Tyrian Heracles, and whose cult was merged with Heracles in the course of the island's Hellenisation. The temple still existed in the time of Herodotus. An eponymous Thassos, son of Phoenix (or of Agenor, as Pausanias reported) was said to have been the leader of the Phoenicians, and to have given his name to the island…

The History of Thassos

On Thassos in around 650 BC, or a little earlier, Greeks from Paros founded a colony on Thassos. A generation or so later, the poet Archilochus, a descendant of these colonists, wrote of casting away his shield during a minor war against an indigenous Thracian tribe. Herodotus says that the best mines on the island were those opened by the Phoenicians on the east side of the island, facing Samothrace…

The History of Thassos

Archilochus described Thassos as "an ass's backbone crowned with wild wood." The island's capital, Thassos, had two harbours. Besides its plentiful gold mines, fine wine, tasty nuts and beautiful marble of Thassos were also well known in antiquity…

The History of Thassos

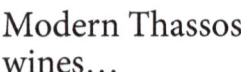
Modern Thassos wines…

Thasian fine wine was well known and on the coins of the period is the head of the wine god Dionysos on one side and bunches of grape on the other. The Island of Thassos was important during the Ionian Revolt against Persia. After the capture of Miletus (494 BC) Histiaeus, the Ionian leader, laid siege to the island…

The History of Thassos

The Ionian siege attack failed, but, warned by the danger, the islander's employed their revenues to build war ships and strengthen their fortifications. This excited the suspicions of the Persians, and Darius compelled them to surrender their ships and pull down their walls. After the defeat of Xerxes the Thasians joined the Delian confederacy; but soon afterwards, the people of the island revolted against those on the mainland once again…

The History of Thassos

The next significant event was that the Athenians defeated them by sea, and, after a siege that lasted more than two years, took the capital, Thassos, probably in 463 BC, and compelled the Thasians to destroy their walls, surrender their ships, pay an indemnity and an annual contribution (in 449 BC this was 21 talents, from 445 BC about 30 talents), and resign their possessions on the mainland. In 411 BC, at the time of the oligarchical revolution at Athens, Thassos again revolted from Athens and received a Lacedaemonian governor; but in 407 BC the partisans of Lacedaemon were expelled, and the Athenians under Thrasybulus were admitted once more…

The History of Thassos

Philip II of Macedonia…

After the battle of Aegospotami in 405 BC, Thassos again fell into the hands of the Lacedaemonians under Lysander who formed a decarchy. But the Athenians must have recovered it, for it formed one of the subjects of dispute between them and Philip II of Macedonia some time later…

The History of Thassos

In the embroilment between Philip V of Macedonia and the Romans, Thassos submitted to Philip, but received its freedom at the hands of the Romans after the Battle of Cynoscephalae (197 BC), and it was still a "free" state at the time of Pliny. Thassos was part of the Eastern Roman Empire, now known as the Byzantine Empire, from 395 BC onwards…

The History of Thassos

According to the 6th-century Synecdemus, Thassos belonged to the province of Macedonia Prima, although by the tenth century De Thematibus claims that it was part of Thracia. The island of Thassos was a major source of marble until the disruption of the trade during the Slavic invasions in the late 6th/7th centuries, and several churches from Late Antiquity have been found on the island. The island of Thassos remained in Roman Byzantine hands for most of the Middle Ages…

The History of Thassos

Thassos functioned as a naval base in the 13th century, under its own doux, and came briefly under the rule of the Genoese Tedisio Zaccaria in 1307–1313 AD. Thassos was captured by the Genoese Gattliusi family in 1434 AD, who surrendered it to the Ottoman Empire in 1455 AD. Under the Ottoman Empire, the island was known as Ottoman Turkish. A brief revolt against Ottoman rule in 1821 AD, at the outbreak of the Greek War of Independence, led by Hatzigiorgis Metaxas, failed. The island was given to Egypt, as a reward for the Egyptians help and support in the War which failed to prevent the creation of the Modern Greek state…

The History of Thassos

Greek hero's and pottery of the early period of Thassos history

Egyptian rule was relatively benign and the island of Thassos became prosperous again. On October 20, 1912 during the First Balkan War, a Greek naval detachment claimed Thassos as part of Greece, which it has remained ever since. In the modern era the Axis occupation (1941–1944) of Thassos, along with the rest of Eastern Macedonia and Thrace, came under Bulgarian control. The Bulgarian government renamed the island "Tasos" and closed its schools as a first step towards forced Bulgarisation…

The History of Thassos

During the second World War Thassos's mountainous terrain facilitated small-scale resistance activity. At the end of the war and the withdrawal of the Axis troops, the island was caught up in the Greek Civil War. Skirmishes and Communist guerrilla attacks continued on Thassos until 1950. This was almost a year after the main hostilities finished on the mainland of Greece. Thassos, the capital, is now informally known as Limenas, or "the port". It is served by a ferry route to and from Keramoti a port close to Kavala International Airport, and has the shortest possible crossing to the island. Susie and I have always stayed at Skala Prinos when we have holidayed on the island. It is 20 km south of Thassos town and it's port has a ferry route to and from Kavala…

The Geography of Thassos

Thassos island is located in the northern Aegean sea approximately 7 km (4 miles) from the northern Greek mainland and 20 kilometres (12 miles) south-east of Kavala, and is of generally rounded shape, without deep bays or significant peninsulas. The terrain is mountainous but not particularly rugged, rising gradually from coast to the centre of the island. The highest peak is Ypsario (Ipsario), at 1,205 metres (3,953 feet), somewhat east of centre. Pine forests cover much of the island's eastern slopes…

The Geography of Thassos

Olive trees on Thassos

Historically, the island's population was chiefly engaged in agriculture and stock breeding, and established villages inland, some of them connected via stairways (known as skalas) to harbours on the sea shore. The local population gradually migrated towards these shoreline settlements as tourism began to develop as an important source of income. Thus, there are several "paired villages" such as Marion–Skala Maries, with the former inland and the latter on the coast. Thassos has in the past been mined for deposits of lead, zinc, silver. gold, copper, iron and marble…

Facts about Thassos

Today you can still see marble being extracted and loaded onto a boat on Thassos. The earliest mining on the island has been dated to around 13,000 BC, when Paleolithic miners dug a shaft at the site of the modern-era Tzines an iron mine for the extraction of limonitic ochre. Mining for base and precious metals started around the 7th century BC with the Phoenicians, followed in the 4th century by the Greeks, then the Romans. Some of the islands olive trees look as if they may have been around at the time!…

Facts about Thassos

Later mines were both open-cast and underground. They mostly exploit the island's numerous karst hosted calamine deposits for their lead and silver. gold, copper and iron were also found on the island and the Byzantines quarried marble on the island…

Facts about Thassos

In the early 20th century, mining companies exploited the island's zinc and lead rich calamine ores, with a yield of around 2 million tonnes, and a processing plant at Limenaria producing zinc oxide. Iron ore was mined on a significant scale from 1954 to 1964, with a yield of around 3 million tonnes. Since 1964, surveys have established the existence of a deep-level zinc-lead deposit, but the main mining activity today on the island is marble quarrying. Susie and I spent half a day during our first visit to the island watching marble being extracted from a hillside quarry. It was fascinating!…

Facts about Thassos

By far the most important economic activity on Thassos today is tourism. The main agricultural products on the island are honey, almonds, olives and olive oil, as well as wine, sheep, goat herding and fishing. Other industries on the island are lumber and mining which includes lead, zinc and marble, especially in the Panagia area where one of the mountains near the Thracian Sea has a large marble quarry which we once visited. The marble quarries in the south (in the area of Aliki), now abandoned, were mined during ancient times…

Out and About on Thassos

Local Communities on Thassos: The Towns and villages with over 100 inhabitants on Thassos are:

- Agios Georgios (149)
- Astris (129)
- Kallirachi (651)
- Kinyra (104)
- Limenaria (2,441)
- Maries (182)
- Ormos Prinou (122)
- Panagia (820)
- Potamia (1,216)
- Potos (688)
- Prinos (1,185)
- Rachoni (365)
- Skala Kallirachis (631)
- Skala Marion (377)
- Skala Rachoniou (206)
- Sotiras (368)
- Thassos (Limenas Thasou) (3,130)
- Theologos (731)

Most of the population is based around Thassos Town and Limenaria…

Out and About on Thassos

The Beaches of Thassos:

Socrates Hotel…

Skala Prinos: Has lots of pine trees and a wonderful beach which is ideal for swimming. We stayed here and it has golden sandy beach and is safe for children.
Pachis: Has crystal clear water that attracts a lot of visitors.
Rachoni: Has a long sandy beach surrounded by pine forest.
Glyadi: Has a beach of golden sand and shallow blue sea.
Skala Potamia and Golden Beach: These have arguably the best beaches on the island. They also have a camping site, lots of restaurants, bars, and nightclubs…

Out and About on Thassos

The Beaches of Thassos:

Giola: Has a natural swimming pool with crystal clear turquoise seawater.
Saliara: Has a white sandy beach (also known as Marble beach).
Paradise, Paradise Beach: is approximately 23 km from Thassos town via the coastal road that circles the Island. Although not signposted itself there is a signpost for the "Paradise Bar on the Beach".
Metalia Beach: Has a fine sandy beach ideal for children and lies 39 km south west of the capital of Thassos.
Glykadi Beach: Has a sandy beach of 150 meters and and offers relaxation in a lush natural environment. It has umbrellas and sunbeds around a beach bar but has no other facilities or infrastructure…

Out and About on Thassos

Places to visit on Thassos:

- Archaeological Museum of Thassos in Thassos Town.
- Polygnotos Vagis Municipal Museum in Potamias.
- Folklore Museum of Limenaria.
- Archangle Michael's Monastery.
- Saint Pateleimon Monastery.
- Monastery of the Assumption.

All of the places above are all well worth a visit during your stay on Thassos…

Out and About on Thassos

Famous People of Thassos:

- Archilochos - (7th century BC) warrior and poet. "You led us a thousand strong at Thassos, fields fattened by corpses."
- Aglaophon - (6th–5th century BC) artist/painter.
- Hegemon of Thassos - (comedian, inventor of parody).
- Leodamas (4th century BC) mathematician.
- Neseus of Thassos (artist/painter).
- Polygotus (mid-5th century BC) artist/painter.
- Stesimbrotos (470 BC - 420 BC) sophist.
- Theagenes (480 BC) Olympic boxer.
- Pankratiast (476 BC) Olympic athlete.
- Polygnotus Vagis - (1892–1965) Thassos-born US sculptor.
- Vassilis Vassilikos (1934) poet and author.
- Demetrios Vassiliades (1958) scholar and author.

The Island of Thassos has produced many famous sons in the past and this tradition, I am sure, will continue into the future…

Exploring Thassos

Golden Beach…

The Beaches of Thassos

Thassos is a favourite with families looking for a beach holiday with an authentic Greek flavour. Beaches are dotted all round the coast of this near-circular island and all are easily reached from the good coast road. The large bay at Golden Beach is the most popular target of package tour firms but good beaches are found all around the coast of Thassos. Limenaria, in the south, has four good beaches while less crowded resorts lie both east and west with good sand and beach facilities. We have holidayed at Skala Prinou but we have always found the time to explore the other resorts and also spend some of our time in the beautiful town of Thassos…

Exploring Thassos

The North-East Coast Beaches on Thassos

The more mountainous east coast of Thassos is covered in a thick pine forest, liberally crossed with hill tracks and fire breaks. The main road from Limenas cuts inland and rises steeply through tortuous bends to the hill villages of Panagia and Potamia before dropping down to Golden Beach and Skala Potamias. Mountain villages such as Panagia and Potamia are a big draw for both ad-hoc visitors and organised coach parties…

Exploring Thassos

Makryammos Beach

The sandy beach at Makryammos lies to the south-east of Thassos Town and looks delightful when approached by boat with steep, pine-clad hills sweeping down to the crescent bay of white sand. Closer inspection, however, reveals a few flaws. An extensive chalet-cum-bungalow complex sits hidden in the wooded hillside and early rising campers will snap up the best beach spots leaving later day visitors to scratch around for what's left. So if you stay here you might need to be up early to get the best spot…

Exploring Thassos

Makryammos Beach

Makryammos is a good family beach of sharp white sand and shallow seawater. It's also a favourite target of day-trip boats which tie up at a breakwater. You also need to be aware that sometimes leaves from the surrounding trees coagulate into great black mounds, slumped like beached whales on the shoreline and attracting swarms of flies. Access from the main road above is through the holiday camp complex where ' Private Property' signs give the impression that Makryammos beach is private - **it is not!**…

Exploring Thassos

Panagia Village

If you take the east road out of Limenas it climbs steeply to the picturesque hill villages of Panagia (pronounced 'Panahia') and Potamis, or Potamia, both big tourist draws thanks to their woodland position above the coastal resorts of Skala Potamias and Golden Beach. In Panagia village centre the cafes and tavernas cluster around a central fountain which gushes water from local springs. Paved village streets head into the hills where there are several good walking trails through wooded hillsides and valleys…

Exploring Thassos

Panagia Village

The more adventurous of you can tackle Mount Ipsarion which looms above the village at over 1,000 metres, the rest can enjoy the lush countryside and walks that offer fine views over the bay below. Booklets with details of local treks are sold at shops in Limenas. Just before Panagia, the road turns a sharp left and drops down to the northern end of Golden Beach…

Exploring Thassos

Alan painting on Thassos with a friend!…

Potamia Village

Potamia, also called Potamis or Potamias, is quieter than Panagia mainly because the main road by-passes the village. It has a soporific air with a few small cafes on the narrow streets. The Greek American artist Polygnotos Vagis was born in Potamias and a small museum devoted to his work can be found in the village…

Exploring Thassos

Potamia Village

The Potamia area is a favourite one for walkers, with many woodland paths up into the hills. Trails also go down to the popular sands at Skala Potamia and Golden Beach, which lie about four kilometres away…

Exploring Thassos

Golden Beach

To get to Golden Beach why not get one of the excursion boats from the quay side at Limenas that head out daily for the long, sandy bay of Golden Beach, or Chrysi Ammoudia to give it its proper Greek title. Golden Beach is very long and deep, with low dunes and large areas of scrub stretched out over the large, flat plain behind. The beach sweeps right around a huge bay, with the hamlet of Chrisi Amoudia at the northern end, ostensibly the beach resort of Panagia, and Skala Potamias to the south, serving Potamia village…

Exploring Thassos

Golden Beach

On Golden Beach the long sandy beach narrows in the middle of the bay and disappear beneath rocks and shingle before re-emerging to the south. Both ends of the beach get fairly crowded while the centre remains almost empty. A road runs along the back of the beach to serve the holiday apartments and occasional tavernas that lie scattered across the flat plain behind…

Exploring Thassos

Skala Potamia

The southern end of Golden Beach opens out into a deep triangle of good white sand edged by a small harbour at the popular resort of Skala Potamia, or Skala Potamias. Some claim the sand at Skala Potamis are the best on Thassos, with its large beach of pale sand sliding gently into shallow blue seawater. This is an ideal bucket and spade location…

Exploring Thassos

Skala Potamia

Skala Potamias has certainly grown very popular with British tour companies in recent years and there has been a spate of new apartment building as a result, although none of it too intrusive as many have been erected in the woodland plain behind the beach. An arcade of tavernas and bars line the back of the Skala Potamis beach, pleasant enough if you don't mind the holiday crowds…

Exploring Thassos

Paradiso Beach

The hamlet of Kinira is located on the east coast about 24 kilometres from Limenas and has two small beaches of white pebble called Loutro and Kinira and also the ruins of a Byzantine baths and an early Christian basilica can be found nearby. South over the headland is the beach at Paradiso, hidden in a beautiful cove and hedged by steep wooded hills. Visitors park under roadside trees at the northern end and follow the steep track down, or they opt to go to the beach using a more gradual gradient at the southern end…

Exploring Thassos

Paradiso Beach

Paradiso beach is deep and long with soft sand and a very shallow shoreline shelf into the sea. The offshore islet of Kinira adds interest and there's a taverna among the dunes at the back of the beach providing sunbeds and basic food and drink. Sheer cliffs at the southern end offer some shade from the afternoon sun and trees encroach on the shallow dunes behind. It was once a big favourite with naturists, the rising popularity of Paradiso has turned it into a family resort beach. Once serenely peaceful, Paradiso now attracts visitors in ever growing numbers…

Exploring Thassos

The South Coast of Thassos

The south coast of Thassos is a very popular holiday area, particularly around Limenaria and at Potos and Pefkari. A lot of visitors prefer to base themselves in this part of Thassos as drives to local beaches tend to be shorter. The landscape is not as impressive as in the north of the island and fortunately the area has now recovered from the effects of a series of devastating forest fires in recent years…

Exploring Thassos

Alyki Beach

Once a secret gem, Alyki is now the target of a large number of daily visitors and a car park has been carved out of the cliff above to accommodate the day trip cars and coaches. Alyki has two small coves, set back-to-back on a narrow wooded promontory. The southern beach is a small crescent of fine sand at the end of a long and narrow inlet of shallow seawater. Half a dozen tavernas sit on a ridge behind nestled beneath shady trees…

Exploring Thassos

Alyki Beach

At Alyki a narrow track leads over the headland to the northern beach, a much smaller and stonier affair, but far less crowded. If you are there during a jaw-dropping wild and windy day you will see spectacular waves swelling through the narrow entrance to the bay and pound onto the stony shore…

Exploring Thassos

Alyki Beach

Between the two beaches of Alyki there are ancient marble quarries and a small archaeological site that includes a couple of early Christian basilicas. Visitors may note the Greek love affair with chain link fencing. Instead of polite notices to keep off the stones there is 8 ft high ugly rusty chain link fencing that wouldn't look out of place around an army camp…

Exploring Thassos

Astris Beach

As you are driving along the coast road south of the monastery at Archangelos, the road winds around several headlands before dropping to a small coastal plain and an excellent sandy beach. Easy to miss on the long straight road Astris is a long strip of golden sand bisected by an outcrop of rock where a ramshackle Greek taverna stands amongst the trees…

Exploring Thassos

Astris Beach

Situated at Astris beach is working boatyard which stands at the northern end of the sands, which are soft and pale and shelve gently into the sea, making this a very good beach for families with young children. Relatively unknown and easy to miss, the beach at Astris rarely gets crowded and makes an ideal spot for those who prefer more peaceful surroundings. There is a small rough area for parking just off the road under the trees. Inland is the village of Astris, noted for its tiny stone built and slate-roofed houses, some of which are available to rent. This is a great bucket and spade family friendly beach!…

Exploring Thassos

Psili Ammos Beach

Marble slabs slope down to the medium sized beach from the roadside car park at the beautiful resort of Psili Ammos. This was once a peaceful spot but nowadays tends to get very busy. This is an ideal family beach and is very popular with people who enjoy sunbathing in an ideal location. This is a good place for those with buckets and spades to play on. A deep arc of rich, golden sand has a couple of tavernas behind, one decked out to resemble a cowboy ranch and belting out all-day pop music; the other, thankfully, is more traditional…

Exploring Thassos

Psili Ammos Beach

The golden sand and beach facilities make Psili Ammos a popular beach for families. The sand, however, dips very sharply into the sea and children must be watched carefully. The steep beach can bring in big waves and there are strong underwater currents. So parents need to keep a sharp eye on their children to ensure they remain safe at all times. This beautiful spot is also favoured by water sports enthusiasts who love the howl of their jet skis and a dive centre sits on the hill. Family and crowds of adults make Psili Ammos a busy, noisy beach in the high season…

Exploring Thassos

Potos Beach

In recent years cushioned cane chairs have sprouted up along the sea front at the popular tourist resort of Potos where more than 30 tavernas, cafes and bars line the short sea wall above a narrow strip of sand. The natural beauty of this beach and its good eating and drinking opportunities makes this a popular place to visit. Rush frond sun umbrellas cover the beach where waiter bar service is available to those who are lucky and can nab a sun lounger. If you like a busy up-market beach then Potos is about as good as it gets on Thassos…

Exploring Thassos

Potos Beach

At Potos the crescent of good sand turns to shingle at the harbour end of the beach. The beach shelves steeply in parts so children must be watched and kept safe at all times. It is a nice place to wandering around the harbour where fishing boats and pleasure boats bob gentle up and down in the sea that makes for a very pleasant experience. Sadly popularity has pushed up the prices, in recent years, but the cafes are colourful and comfortable while the many boats pulled onto the beach near the harbour adds even more colour and interest…

Exploring Thassos

Potos Village

The village of Potos is a maze of back streets full of shops and cafes. Cars are forced to a crawl in the narrow, crowded streets so visitors park on the main road and walk to the beach. This is a great place to sit with a drink and watch the world go by. To the south of Potos is Ossegromos Beach, small and little visited, where a small stretch of sharp, white sand is surrounded by trees…

Exploring Thassos

Pefkari Beach

On Pefkari beach paddle boats, surfboards and jet skis are prominently parked on the manicured white sands. These are all clues, if they are needed, to the popularity of the beach resort at Pefkari. Gently shelving sand and shallow seawater makes it an ideal spot for families with children. The nearby headland offers splendid cliff side walk's. So grab your bucket and spade and walking boots and enjoy all that this resort has to offer…

Exploring Thassos

Pefkari Beach

Lots of tavernas and cafes line both sides of the shady, quiet lane that runs along the back of Pefkari beach. The busy main road bypasses the village completely. The beach is long and deep with soft white sand that is kept very clean by the taverna owners. There are masses of sunbeds and a wide range of water sports on offer. A large neighbouring hotel complex ensures that Pefkari beach stays heavily crowded in the high season…

Exploring Thassos

Metalia Beach

Metalia beach lies just east of the big south coast resort of Limenaria. It has a small beach bar and an abandoned World War Two factory, with derelict smelting chimneys as a backdrop. Many people find that the beach offers somewhere somewhat quieter than the nearby larger resort beaches. This makes it very popular with families looking for somewhere for the children to play safely on the beach…

Exploring Thassos

Metalia Beach

Metalia is a quiet and attractive beach and certainly different from its nearby neighbours. So much so that some rate this amongst the best beaches on Thassos. Metalia is a notably quieter alternative to Limenaria and worth exploring if you are staying in the area…

Exploring Thassos

Limenaria Resort

Limenaria is the second biggest resort on the island after Limenas. It has a long waterfront promenade which is backed by dozens of tavernas, bars, cafes and shops. The west end of the promenade is lined with large boulders and a scruffy, narrow beach. The eastern end has a small arc of pleasant sand overlooked by a busy road and a small, square shaped harbour full of fishing boats…

Exploring Thassos

Limenaria Resort

Limenaria is a good base for a holiday with several good beaches nearby. Hillside mansions built by German mining bosses at the turn of the century add some character to what is a fairly humdrum resort. The restaurants in the resort have a good reputation for good food. Tourists tend to use Limenaria as a base to explore the south of Thassos and there are good walks in the pine-carpeted hills…

Exploring Thassos

Trypiti Beach

Trypiti, sometimes spelt Tripiti, lies to the west of Limenaria, about two kilometres from the resort and well marked from the main road. There is no village here, just a long, deep and sandy beach that's handy for those staying in Limenaria and an improvement on the relatively poor town beaches. The sands sweep right around a huge bay with a dirt track behind for much of its length where cars can be parked just about anywhere. Beach bars at both ends serve up the basic food and drink requirements for the weary holidaymaker…

Exploring Thassos

Trypiti Beach

To the west of Trypiti beach is a small sea cave and shallow pool that children can enjoy, although it shelves deeply inside the cave and waves come crashing in on windy days. The sand also shelves rather steeply into the sea and there can be clumps of seaweed now and then but Trypiti is still a big pleasant beach with sunbeds at both ends, near the beach bars…

Exploring Thassos

West Coast Beaches

The west coast of Thassos is much flatter than the east, with rolling farmland and small inland hamlets. The road has fewer bends and resorts are much easier to reach. Beaches may not be as good as those in the east but there are some very pleasant resorts on this part of the coast. Less crowded and less tainted by tourism it offers an attractive addition to what Thassos island' has to offer the holidaymaker…

Exploring Thassos

Skala Maries Resort

Skala Maries is a somewhat isolated resort that is set in a deep crescent of a bay. Accommodation in the resort climbs up a small hill overlooking the sandy beach…

Exploring Thassos

Skala Maries Resort

Although Skala Maries benefits from a crescent of sand and scrub. The local practice of pulling the occasional rotting hulk of a boat up onto the foreshore adds nothing to the resort. When I last visited the resort I found that the large number of derelict and semi-built houses added nothing to the general air of neglect. A pity as the setting is very nice…

Exploring Thassos

Skala Kalirachis Harbour

Skala Kalirachis is basically a huge harbour with a couple of small scraps of sand at either end. A wide concrete road runs the length of the quay side backed by houses and apartments and ending at the northern end in a handkerchief of a scruffy sand and shingle beach, hemmed in by a high concrete wall…

Exploring Thassos

Skala Kalirachis Harbour

To the south of Skala Kalirachis harbour is another small scrap of sand on the other side of the jetty, a little more substantial this time with a few sunbeds but it is not a great deal more inviting than the other…

Exploring Thassos

Skala Sotiros Beach

Skala Sotiros, sometimes called Skala Sotirou, has a very pleasant beach located down a side street branching off the main road through the village and is well worth a visit…

Exploring Thassos

Skala Sotiros Beach

Skala Sotiros village is little more than a ribbon of houses strung along the main busy road but the beach has a good stretch of sand sprinkled with sunbeds near the short jetty in front of the main taverna. The southern end of the beach quickly turns to shingle and stone but there is good swathe of sand at the northern end and the seawater here is sheltered and shallow and ideal for children to play and build sand-castles!…

Exploring Thassos

Dasyllio Prinou Beach

Dasyllio Prinou, or Dasyllios Prinos, is the name now given to the whole area and includes a long beach backed by several resort hotels as well as a very large camping site. It can be approached from Skala Sotiros or by turning left at the port in Skala Prinou and following the narrow coast road through the woods and around the headland…

Exploring Thassos

Dasyllio Prinou Resort

Dasyllio Prinou stretches from the main port of Skala Prinou for two kilometres south with a 300-space camping site that is the biggest on Thassos and has facilities that include showers and toilets. As the resort has grown more popular in recent years a number of smart hotels have also been built here…

Exploring Thassos

Dasyllio Prinou Resort

Around Dasyllio Prinou it is heavily wooded, with about 250 varieties of trees recorded here. But then, Dasyllio is the Greek name for little forest and the trees reach right down to the shore and the very long and sandy beach…

Exploring Thassos

Skala Prinou Port

When we have holidayed on Thassos we have always stayed at the Hotel Socrates in the resort of Skala Prinou and found it to be a first-rate beach resort. We have caught the ferry from here to Kavala and the local bus into Thassos Town several times per holiday. We found it was the perfect base for us and it shows that Skala Prinos, is not just a place to catch a ferry…

Exploring Thassos

Skala Prinou Port

In fairness we found that although it may be a fine base for exploring the rest of the island it is, in fact, little more than a bus and ferry stop for many. That said, recent efforts have been made to smarten the place up with new paving and roads as well as a clutch of cafes, tavernas and shops to catch the passing ferry trade. Also on the plus side is a long, narrow beach that stretches north with a shallow sloping bay backed by a line of trees but the beach is scruffy sand and stone and not particularly attractive…

Exploring Thassos

Pachis Beach

Just north of Skala Rachonis is Pachis Beach, a long stretch of golden sand backed by many tamarisk trees with plenty of parking. A small hotel sits on the road and a dirt track leads down to the beach. We have had several nice days on this beach during our stays on the island…

Exploring Thassos

Pachis Beach

At Pachis beach there are a couple of large tavernas and some beach bars at one end of the beach but many visitors opt for the other end of the beach where there is the best of the sand, and a pleasant cantina under the trees…

Exploring Thassos

Pachis Beach

On Pachis beach the sand is soft and golden and it's fairly shallow offshore and good for families with children. Tamarisk trees and pines provide plenty of good natural shade. Over the headland to the north is the tiny beach of Glyferoni at the head of a small bay and best reached from the main road down an unmarked path. Please note that it has no facilities…

Exploring Thassos

Glyfada Area Beaches

The road from Pachis heading towards Glyfada follows the coast around the headland before turning south-east and back towards Thassos Town. It passes a few small beaches. One is called Perasama which has small sandy cove with a summer beach cantina. There are tiny patches of sand at Papalimani and Agia Irini on either side of a rocky headland…

Exploring Thassos

Glyfada Beach

The road eventually reaches Glyfada where there is a quiet sand strip in front of a hotel. It is only a short walk from Limenas but the road is steeply uphill. The sands are pleasant enough, although rather narrow in places. The trees offer plenty of shade and there are facilities and parking available at the hotel…

Exploring Thassos

Nysteri Beach

A small but splendid tree-lined beach lies below the hotel at Nysteri, just outside Thassos and a kilometre east from Glyfada. The hotel caters mainly for German guests and has a small outdoor terrace bar overlooking the beach…

Exploring Thassos

Nysteri Beach

There is plenty of parking on a large patch of ground off the main road at the eastern end of the beach where a rough track leads down through woodland to the shore. Nysteri has a fine sandy beach with shallow seawater and sunbeds laid out by the hotel and some changing cubicles. Trees behind the sand offer plenty of good shade and a small cantina opens in the woods during the high season…

Thassos Town

Thassos Town, known locally as Limenas, is the island's main town, but not its main port which lies to the east at Ormos Prinou. Everyone who visits this island should spend several days of their holiday visiting this beautiful town. The town was once split into two with a pretty port to the east and a cement wasteland to the west. A great deal has been done to improve this area in recent years and widen its appeal…

Thassos Town

Susie, our daughter Ginny and I would often spend all day wandering around this lovely town sampling all it has to offer as we went. The marble-laden lorries that once heaved through the town centre now go west and the new port has been re-paved and planted with attractive shrubs. The prettiest part of Thassos Town is still the old port where a traffic ban paves the way for taverna tables and street stalls piled high with Thassos honey…

Thassos Town

The Old Port enjoys a warm, rustic atmosphere, where the brightly painted fishing boats bob against quays strewn with fishing nets. This truly is a idyllic spot for the weary traveller to sit at an open air table and enjoy a cold drink and something to eat while enjoying the wonderful views….

Thassos Town

Susie, Ginny and I enjoyed visiting Thassos Town so much that we said next time we visit the island we will base ourselves in the town. The beach lies east of the old harbour and it's long and deep. Smartened up now and then with lorry-loads of sand, it is still a very pleasant spot with shallow water and sunbeds. Tavernas line the road behind the beach where attractive tamarisk trees also offer plenty of chance of natural shade…

Thassos Town

Thassos Town has several archaeological sites. The Agora, next to the revamped Archaeological Museum has impressive Roman foundations while an amphitheatre in the hills above hosts summer performances against a backdrop of fabulous views over the bay. On the hill ridge above are well-restored city walls and the remains of an Acropolis, with temples to Apollo and Athena…

Thassos Town

West of Thassos Town a coastal track leads to a string of small beach coves known collectively as Agios Vasilios. Each cove has a beach bar, taverna or small hotel and is an attractive lure for those who want to stay close to town. Having exhausted ourselves wandering around Thassos Town, in the next and last chapter, we will take a rest and enjoy looking at all the beauty that is Thassos in Colour…

Thassos in Colour

The Paradise Greek Island of Thassos

Thassos in Colour

The Paradise Greek Island of Thassos

Thassos in Colour

The Paradise Greek Island of Thassos

Thassos in Colour

The Paradise Greek Island of Thassos

Thassos in Colour

The Paradise Greek Island of Thassos

Thassos in Colour

The Paradise Greek Island of Thassos

Thassos in Colour

The Paradise Greek Island of Thassos

Thassos in Colour

The Paradise Greek Island of Thassos

Thassos in Colour

The Paradise Greek Island of Thassos

Thassos in Colour

The Paradise Greek Island of Thassos

Thassos in Colour

The Paradise Greek Island of Thassos

Thassos in Colour

The Paradise Greek Island of Thassos

Thassos in Colour

The Paradise Greek Island of Thassos

Thassos in Colour

The Paradise Greek Island of Thassos

Thassos in Colour

The Paradise Greek Island of Thassos

Thassos in Colour

The Paradise Greek Island of Thassos

Thassos in Colour

The Paradise Greek Island of Thassos

Thassos in Colour

The Paradise Greek Island of Thassos

Thassos in Colour

The Paradise Greek Island of Thassos

Thassos in Colour

The Paradise Greek Island of Thassos

Thassos in Colour

The Paradise Greek Island of Thassos

Thassos in Colour

The Paradise Greek Island of Thassos

Thassos in Colour

The Paradise Greek Island of Thassos

Thassos in Colour

The Paradise Greek Island of Thassos

Thassos in Colour

The Paradise Greek Island of Thassos

Thassos in Colour

The Paradise Greek Island of Thassos

Thassos in Colour

The Paradise Greek Island of Thassos

Thassos in Colour

The Paradise Greek Island of Thassos

Thassos in Colour

The Paradise Greek Island of Thassos

Thassos in Colour

The Paradise Greek Island of Thassos

Thassos in Colour

The Paradise Greek Island of Thassos

Thassos in Colour

The Paradise Greek Island of Thassos

Thassos in Colour

The Paradise Greek Island of Thassos

Thassos in Colour

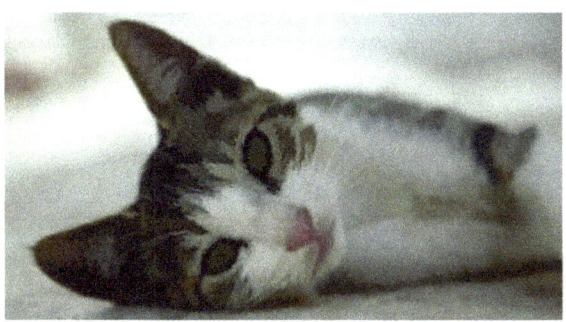

The Paradise Greek Island of Thassos

Thassos in Colour

The Paradise Greek Island of Thassos

Thassos in Colour

The Paradise Greek Island of Thassos

Thassos in Colour

The Paradise Greek Island of Thassos

Thassos in Colour

The Paradise Greek Island of Thassos

Thassos in Colour

The Paradise Greek Island of Thassos

Thassos in Colour

The Paradise Greek Island of Thassos

Thassos in Colour

The Paradise Greek Island of Thassos

Thassos in Colour

The Paradise Greek Island of Thassos

Thassos in Colour

The Paradise Greek Island of Thassos

Thassos in Colour

The Paradise Greek Island of Thassos

Thassos in Colour

The Paradise Greek Island of Thassos

Thassos in Colour

The Paradise Greek Island of Thassos

Thassos in Colour

The Paradise Greek Island of Thassos

Thassos in Colour

The Paradise Greek Island of Thassos

Thassos in Colour

The Paradise Greek Island of Thassos

Thassos in Colour

The Paradise Greek Island of Thassos

Thassos in Colour

The Paradise Greek Island of Thassos

Thassos in Colour

The Paradise Greek Island of Thassos

Thassos in Colour

The Paradise Greek Island of Thassos

Thassos in Colour

The Paradise Greek Island of Thassos

Thassos in Colour

The Paradise Greek Island of Thassos

Thassos in Colour

The Paradise Greek Island of Thassos

Thassos in Colour

The Paradise Greek Island of Thassos

Thassos in Colour

The Paradise Greek Island of Thassos

Thassos in Colour

The Paradise Greek Island of Thassos

Thassos in Colour

The Paradise Greek Island of Thassos

Thassos in Colour

The Paradise Greek Island of Thassos

Thassos in Colour

The Paradise Greek Island of Thassos

Thassos in Colour

The Paradise Greek Island of Thassos

Thassos in Colour

The Paradise Greek Island of Thassos

Thassos in Colour

The Paradise Greek Island of Thassos

Thassos in Colour

The Paradise Greek Island of Thassos

Thassos in Colour

The Paradise Greek Island of Thassos

Thassos in Colour

The Paradise Greek Island of Thassos

Thassos in Colour

The Paradise Greek Island of Thassos

Thassos in Colour

The Paradise Greek Island of Thassos

Thassos in Colour

The Paradise Greek Island of Thassos

Thassos in Colour

The Paradise Greek Island of Thassos

Thassos in Colour

The Paradise Greek Island of Thassos

Thassos in Colour

The Paradise Greek Island of Thassos

Thassos in Colour

The Paradise Greek Island of Thassos

Thassos in Colour

The Paradise Greek Island of Thassos

Thassos in Colour

The Paradise Greek Island of Thassos

Thassos in Colour

The Paradise Greek Island of Thassos

Thassos in Colour

The Paradise Greek Island of Thassos

Thassos in Colour

The Paradise Greek Island of Thassos

Thassos in Colour

The Paradise Greek Island of Thassos

Thassos in Colour

The Paradise Greek Island of Thassos

Thassos in Colour

The Paradise Greek Island of Thassos

Thassos in Colour

The Paradise Greek Island of Thassos

Thassos in Colour

The Paradise Greek Island of Thassos

Thassos in Colour

The Paradise Greek Island of Thassos

Thassos in Colour

The Paradise Greek Island of Thassos

Thassos in Colour

The Paradise Greek Island of Thassos

Thassos in Colour

The Paradise Greek Island of Thassos

Thassos in Colour

The Paradise Greek Island of Thassos

Thassos in Colour

The Paradise Greek Island of Thassos

Thassos in Colour

The Paradise Greek Island of Thassos

Thassos in Colour

The Paradise Greek Island of Thassos

Thassos in Colour

The Paradise Greek Island of Thassos

Thassos in Colour

The Paradise Greek Island of Thassos

Thassos in Colour

The Paradise Greek Island of Thassos

Thassos in Colour

The Paradise Greek Island of Thassos

Thassos in Colour

The Paradise Greek Island of Thassos

Thassos in Colour

The Paradise Greek Island of Thassos

Thassos in Colour

The Paradise Greek Island of Thassos

Thassos in Colour

The Paradise Greek Island of Thassos

Thassos in Colour

The Paradise Greek Island of Thassos

Thassos in Colour

The Paradise Greek Island of Thassos

Thassos in Colour

The Paradise Greek Island of Thassos

Thassos in Colour

The Paradise Greek Island of Thassos

Thassos in Colour

The Paradise Greek Island of Thassos

Thassos in Colour

The Paradise Greek Island of Thassos

Thassos in Colour

The Paradise Greek Island of Thassos

Thassos in Colour

The Paradise Greek Island of Thassos

Thassos in Colour

The Paradise Greek Island of Thassos

Thassos in Colour

The Paradise Greek Island of Thassos

Thassos in Colour

As we close this Chapter on "**Thassos in Colour**" it is time for us to also leave the Greek paradise island of Thassos. Susie and I have enjoyed our summer holidays here in the past and hope to go again in the future but it is now time for Susie and I to say goodbye. So until the next time happy holidays and I hope you have enjoyed our journey together around the Island of Thassos and I hope that you will also get a chance to visit the island yourself real soon…

Acknowledgement

I would like to acknowledge and thank ALL the people of Thassos who have helped make all our family holidays to their beautiful island over the years such a positive and happy experience.

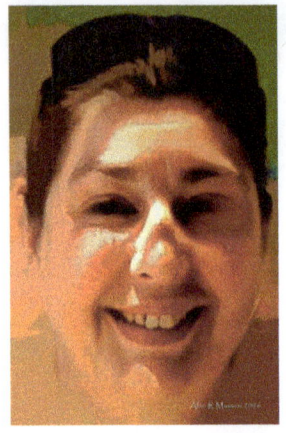  

Copyright © 2020 Alan R. Massen

Finally, as the sun goes down, for me, the most important thing to ensure that you enjoy your holiday to the full is that you have someone to share your experiences with. I am so lucky. I have my wife Susie as my companion on all our Mediterranean and UK holidays. Her smile and enthusiasm has made every day of our stays at home and abroad very enjoyable and memorable. For that I say a big **THANK YOU to SUSIE xxx**…

product-compliance